JOURNAL FOR THE STUDY OF THE OLD TESTAMENT
SUPPLEMENT SERIES
1

Editors
David J A Clines
Philip R Davies
David M Gunn

Department of Biblical Studies
The University of Sheffield
Sheffield S10 2TN
England

I, He, We, & They

A Literary Approach to Isaiah 53

David J A Clines

JOURNAL FOR THE
STUDY OF THE
OLD TESTAMENT

SUPPLEMENT SERIES 1

First published by JSOT Press 1976
Reprint edition by JSOT Press 1983

Copyright © 1976, 1983 JSOT Press

ISSN 0309-0787
ISBN 0 905774 00 0

Published by
JSOT Press
Department of Biblical Studies
The University of Sheffield
Sheffield S10 2TN
England

Printed and bound in Great Britain by
Redwood Burn Ltd.
Trowbridge, Wiltshire
1983

CONTENTS

BIBLIOGRAPHY

J. Begrich, *Studien zu Deuterojesaja* (ed. W. Zimmerli; München: Chr. Kaiser, 1963)

T.K. Cheyne, *The Book of the Prophet Isaiah* (Polychrome Bible; London: James Clarke, 1898)

M. Dahood, "Phoenician Elements in Isaiah 52:13 - 53:12", in *Near Eastern Studies in Honor of William Foxwell Albright* (ed. H. Goedicke; Baltimore and London: Johns Hopkins, 1971) 63-73

P.A.H. de Boer, *Second-Isaiah's Message* (OTS 11; Leiden: Brill, 1956)

G.R. Driver, "Isaiah 52:13 — 53:12: the Servant of the Lord", in *In Memoriam Paul Kahle* (ed. M. Black and G. Fohrer; BZAW 103; Berlin: Töpelmann, 1968) 90-105

B. Duhm, *Das Buch Jesaia* (Göttingen: Vandenhoeck und Ruprecht, 5th edn., 1968)

G. Fohrer, *Das Buch Jesaja,* Bd. 3 (Zürcher Bibelkommentare; Zürich and Stuttgart: Zwingli, 1964)

E.J. Kissane, *The Book of Isaiah*, vol. 2 (Dublin: Browne and Nolan, 1943)

K. Marti, *Das Buch Jesaja* (KHAT 10; Tübingen: Mohr, 1900)

J.L. McKenzie, *Second Isaiah* (AB; Garden City, N.Y.: Doubleday, 1968)

J. Morgenstern, "The suffering servant — a new solution", *VT* 11 1961) 292-320, 406-431

J. Muilenburg, "Isaiah, Chapters 40 - 66", in *The Interpreter's Bible* (ed. G.A. Buttrick; New York and Nashville: Abingdon, 1956) vol. 5

C.R. North, *The Second Isaiah* (Oxford: Clarendon Press, 1964)

H.M. Orlinsky, *The So-Called "Servant of the Lord" and "Suffering Servant" in Second Isaiah* (VT Sup XIV; Leiden: Brill, 1967)

D.F. Payne, "The Servant of the Lord: Language and Identification", *EvQ* 43 (1971) 131-43

L. Rignell, *A Study of Isaiah Ch. 40 - 55* (Lunds Universitets Arsskrift. N.F. Avd. 1. Bd 52. Nr. 5; Lund : Gleerup, 1956)

J. Skinner, *The Book of the Prophet Isaiah, chapters XL - LXVI* (Cambridge: University Press, revised edn, 1917)

N.H. Snaith, *Isaiah 40 - 66. A Study of the Teaching of the Second Isaiah and its Consequences* (VT Sup XIV; Leiden: Brill, 1967)

G.W. Wade, *The Book of the Prophet Isaiah* (Westminster Commentaries; London: Methuen, 2nd edn., 1929)

C. Westermann, *Isaiah 40 - 66* (London: SCM, 1969)

O.C. Whitehouse, *Isaiah XL - LXVI* (Century Bible; Edinburgh: T. and T. Clark, 1908)

R.N. Whybray, *Isaiah 40 -66* (New Century Bible; London: Oliphants, 1975)

D. Winton Thomas, "A Consideration of Isaiah LIII in the Light of Recent Textual and Philological Study", in *De Mari à Qumran. L'Ancien Testament. Son milieu. Ses écrits. Ses relectures juives. Hommage à Mgr J. Coppens* (ed. H. Cazelles; Bibliotheca Ephemeridum Theologicarum Lovaniensium XXIV; Gembloux: J. Duculot, and Paris: P. Lethielleux, 1969) 119 - 26

1. THE SAID : TEXT AND TRANSLATION

1. The said : text and translation

I use the term "Isaiah 53" as a convenient, though loose, heading for the poem Isaiah 52:13 - 53:12.[1] The title, the "Fourth Servant Song" is best avoided since it raises too many extraneous issues, and, what is worse, determines that we approach the poem with an already fixed frame of reference. That the poem is a unit I take for granted, in spite of some recent dissentients;[2] P.—E. Dion's arguments for its unity are impressive enough:

> The initial *hinneh* ("behold") suggests a new departure; from this
> verse onward, the Exodus imagery used in 52:11-12 disappears;
> 52:13-15 and 53:11-12 form two speeches of Yahweh framing
> the whole of chapter 53 and corresponding well to one another:
> in each Yahweh says "my servant" and draws attention to the
> contrast between the humiliation and the exaltation of the *'ebed*.[3]

A thorough treatment of the textual and translational difficulties of the poem would demand a monograph to itself. Here I have space only for a version embodying the understanding of the poem set forward in the present work, together with some justificatory and explanatory notes.

I

52:13 *See, my servant: his wisdom prospers!*
he is lifted up;
he is exalted;
he is raised to the heights!
14 *Once the populace were appalled when they saw him -*
so disfigured he looked,
he seemed less than human -
15 *but now the crowds are astonished at him,*
kings stand speechless before him;
for they see something never told before,
they ponder something never before heard.

---

1 See the bibliography for details of works referred to by their author's name alone.

2 Orlinsky, 17-23; Whybray, 169.

3 P.-E. Dion, "Les chants du Serviteur de Yahweh et quelques passages apparentés d'Is. 40-55. Un essai sur leurs limites précises et sur leurs origines respectives", *Bib* 51 (1970) 17-38 (19).

II

53:1 *Who would have believed what we have heard?*
            Where has God's power ever been seen - but here?
2 *He grew up among us, like a sapling -*
            like a plant rooted in dry ground.
   So he had no beauty,
            no splendour to attract us,
            no grace to charm us.
3 *Spurned and withdrawing from human society,*
            he was a man who suffered;
            pain was his close acquaintance.
   Like one who must hide his face from us
            he was despised;
            we held him of no account.

III

4 *And yet -*
   they were our sufferings that weighed on him;
            our pains were the burden he bore.
   While we -
   We counted him smitten by God,
            struck down by God,
            humiliated by God!
5 *But he -*
   he was pierced by our rebellions,
            crushed by our misdeeds;
   his burden was the suffering that made us whole,
            he endured pain that brought healing to us.
6 *While we -*
   we were the guilty;
            we had strayed like sheep,
            each going his own way.
   But God!
   God burdened him
            with the punishment for the guilt of us all.

IV

7   *He was oppressed;*
        he was struck down.
    He said nothing.
    He was taken away -
        like a sheep to slaughter,
        like a ewe to the shearers.
    He said nothing.
    He was silent.
8   *He was arrested;*
        he was sentenced.
    He was taken away;
        no one raised a protest at his fate.
    He was cut off from the land of life,
        struck down because of the guilt of his people.
9   *He was assigned a grave with the wicked,*
        a burial place with criminals -
    for he had practised non-violence,
        and had never spoken dishonestly!

V

10 *It is God who purposes the suffering;*
        God puts him to grief.
    When his life is offered for the guilt of others,
        he sees his offspring,
        he gains vitality,
        by him Yahweh's plans prosper.
11 *After he has drunk deep of affliction,*
        is satiated with suffering,
    he is proved innocent before the multitudes;
        it is their guilt he bears.

VI

12 *So I rank him among the great,*
        and he may take a hero's portion,
    because he exposed himself to death,

> *letting himself be taken as a sinner;*
> *and all the while he was suffering the guilt of many,*
> *and intervening for wrongdoers.*

52:13 On the tenses here and elsewhere, see below, chapter 3 f. In *śkl* both meanings "be wise" and "prosper" are probably combined,[4] since the servant's success springs directly from his knowledge or experience.[5] I retain the traditional rendering of *'abdî* "my servant", only because the alternatives are too specific. Properly speaking, since these are presumably the words of Yahweh, *'abdî* is "my worshipper"; but "servant" or "slave" is preferable to preserve the contrast with the *m^elākîm* of the nations (52:15).[6]

52:14 The usual emendations of *'āleykā* to *'alāyw*[7] and *mišhat* to *mošhāt*[8] (cf. BHS) I accept, but find it unnecessary to transfer 14b to follow 53:2.[9]

52:15 Driver recently offered a defence of the derivation of *yazzeh* from *nzh* II, cognate with Arab. *nazâ* "he leapt", hence "he caused to leap, startled", here.[10] There is no need however, to read the intransitive *yizzeh* to approximate more closely to LXX *thaumasontai*. Snaith is perhaps correct in claiming that *yiqp^esû* does not merely mean "shut their mouths", but "place the hand over

---

4 Cf. Whybray, 169; Rignell, 79 ("show insight"). Certainly it is the wisdom of the servant of Yahweh that is particularly fastened on in later interpretations of the figure of Isa. 53 (cf. F.F. Bruce, *Biblical Exegesis in the Qumran Texts* (London: Tyndale, 1960) 58). For further interpretation of Isa. 53 see M.J. Suggs, "Wisdom of Solomon 2$_{10}$-5: A Homily Based on the Fourth Servant Song", *JBL* 76 (1957) 26-33.

5 Especially if that is what *da'tô* means in 53:11; see Rignell, "Isa. LII 13 - LIII 12", *VT* 3 (1953) 87-93 (87f.).

6 See de Boer, 112f.

7 So e.g. Marti, 345; Duhm, 394. Perhaps, however, emendation is not actually necessary (cf. de Boer, 113; North, 227; Whybray, 170).

8 So BHS; Dahood, 65. The suggestion of Y. Komlosh, "The Countenance of the Servant of the Lord, Was it Marred?", *JQR* 65 (1975) 217-20, to read *mšhtw* (from **mšhh*, cf. Aram. *mšha'* "measure") and to translate the line "His stature more than any man, and his visage and form unlike the sons of men", results in an improbable metrical pattern of 4+2+4.

9 As Marti, 347; Duhm, 396; Whybray, 169f.; NEB.

10 Driver, 92; cf. BDB *s.v.* Snaith, 161, offers the interesting translation "cause them to leap to their feet", comparing Job 29:8f., which uses similar language about gestures of respect; but is "to leap to one's feet" anything more than an English idiom?

the mouth and clutch it".[11]

53:1   Though it is not recognised by commentators, 1b must be, like 1a, a rhetorical question expecting a negative answer.[12] That is, the poet is denying that God's arm (power)[13] has ever been truly "revealed" previously.[14] It is of course effectively revealed in the case of the servant of Yahweh; hence my addition " − but here?".

53:2   Driver's defence of MT $l^e p\bar{a}n\bar{a}yw$ understood as "straight up"[15] has received some support,[16] but his primary parallel, with 1 Sam. 5:4 (Dagon is $n\bar{o}p\bar{e}l\ l^e p\bar{a}n\bar{a}yw$), is no parallel at all, since that phrase means "fallen on his face", i.e. not backwards, rather than "straight in front of him".[17] It is also doubtful what the point of stressing that the servant "shot straight up"[18] is, or even that he "grew up before the LORD" (NEB).[19] Since what is primarily in view in this strophe is the relation between the servant and the

11 Snaith, 161; for the gesture, see B. Couroyer, " 'Mettre sa main sur sa bouche' en Egypte et dans la Bible", *RB* 67 (1960) 197-209; to which add, for a Mesopotamian example, M. Pope, *Job* (AB; New York: Doubleday, 1965), 157.

12 North, 236, for example, says this of the first question, but makes no comment on the second. Wade, 338, interprets: "Who could have divined such a signal manifestation of the Lord's power . . . as that which has been witnessed in the release and restoration of Israel?"; but it is not a question in 1b of whether anyone could have guessed that it was Yahweh's doing, but of whether Yahweh has ever truly displayed *(glh)* his power previously. Kissane, 185, remarks that 1b is "usually taken as equivalent to a negative statement" (a view which I have been unable to find explicitly stated in the commentaries), and argues in effect that 1b is not a rhetorical question, but expresses the nations' enquiry about the servant. Fohrer, 162, recognizes 1b as a rhetorical question, but refers it too closely to the work of the prophet himself, i.e., no one has yet seen God's power revealed in the activity of the prophet himself.

13 Not "grace" or "salvation" as H.L. Ginsberg has strongly argued, "The Arm of Yhwh in Isaiah 51-63 and the Text of Isa. 53:10-11", *JBL* 77 (1958) 152-56.

14 For the claim that previous acts of God are nothing by comparison with what the poet sees happening in his own days, cf. 43:18 "Remember not the former things".

15 G.R. Driver, "Linguistic and Textual Problems: Isaiah I-XXXIX", *JTS* 38 (1937) 36-50 (48).

16 E.g. Winton Thomas, 121; R.P. Gordon, "Isaiah LIII 2", *VT* 20 (1970) 491f., adducing some Syriac parallels, which are not strictly apposite, since in their case some such phrase is explicable from the literal sense.

17 Driver himself apparently had second thoughts about his suggestion, for in his latest article he translated, "in his sight he shot up like a sapling" (p. 103).

18 Winton Thomas, 119.

19 By itself it would mean that "Yahweh was aware of the Servant's misfortunes, yet appeared to do nothing to remedy them" (Whybray, 173f.), but that does not seem apposite at this point in the poem.

"we" (see below, chapter 3 a), I am inclined to adopt the admittedly conjectural emendation $l^e p\bar{a}n\hat{e}n\hat{u}$ "before us". The recent emendation of G. Schwarz $mippin\bar{a}$, "from a battlement", seems distinctly less probable.[20] Certainly $\check{s}\bar{o}re\check{s}$ means in the present context "stock" or "stem" rather than simply "root".[21]

53:3 I take $h^a dal$ $\,{}^{\prime}\hat{i}\check{s}\hat{i}m$, following Winton Thomas' comparison of hdl with Arab. $hadala$ "to hold back from, leave, abstain",[22] as active, not passive. The servant knows his own ugliness and voluntarily withdraws from human society to avoid giving offence by his disfigurement (52:14). The same significance attaches to $mast\bar{e}r$ $p\bar{a}n\hat{i}m$, if we repoint $mast\bar{e}r$ as $mastir$ (defective spelling for $mast\hat{i}r$, hiph. participle; cf. 1QIs^a $mstyr$).[23] Another possible translation of the phrase $w\hat{i}d\hat{u}a^{\boldsymbol{\cdot}}$ $h\bar{o}l\hat{i}$ is "and humiliated, or, humbled by suffering" (cf. NEB "tormented and humbled by suffering"), if the proposal of Driver is followed,[24] that the verb $yada^{\boldsymbol{\cdot}}$ here is not "to know" but $yada^{\boldsymbol{\cdot}}$ II "to be quiet, still, at ease; to be submissive, humiliated". It is difficult to decide between the two possibilities. The existence of $yada^{\boldsymbol{\cdot}}$ II seems well enough established;[25] both meanings suit the context; the resultant problem of ambiguity[26] might therefore suggest that the poet will have used

20 "»... wie ein Reis vor ihm«?", *ZAW* 83 (1971) 256f.

21 See H.L. Ginsberg, "'Roots below and fruit above' and related matters", in *Hebrew and Semitic Studies presented to G.R. Driver* (ed. D. Winton Thomas and W.D. McHardy; Oxford: Clarendon Press, 1963) 72-76; and A.R. Millard, "Isaiah 53:2", *Tyndale Bulletin* 20 (1969) 127.

22 D. Winton Thomas, "Some Observations on the Hebrew Root hdl", *VTSup* 4 (1957) 8-16; *id.*, "Isaiah LIII" 122; followed by Driver, 92f.; NEB. Less convincing is the interpretation of P.J. Calderone, associating $had\bar{e}t$ with Arab. $hadula$ "be fat, dull" and translating "the most senseless [religiously speaking] of men" ("Supplementary Note on HDL-II", *CBQ* 24 [1962] 412-19 [416-19]); it is followed by Dahood, 64, 66.

23 So Winton Thomas, 123; Dahood, 67. Less probable are the translations "like one who causes (others) to hide (their) faces from him" or "as if (Yahweh) were hiding his face from him" (J. Heller; see Whybray, 174f.).

24 Driver, "Linguistic and Textual Problems: Isaiah I-XXXIX" 49. The existence of $y\bar{a}da^{c}$ II was first postulated by D. Winton Thomas, "The root yd^{c} in Hebrew", *JTS* 35 (1934) 298-306, and he subsequently acknowledged its presence both here and in v. 11 (*JTS* 38 [1937] 404f.; "Isaiah LIII" 122f., 126).

25 See the discussion by J.A. Emerton, "A Consideration of Some Alleged Meanings of yd^{c} in Hebrew", *JSS* 15 (1970) 145-80.

26 See further D.F. Payne, "Old Testament Exegesis and the Problem of Ambiguity", *ASTI* 5 (1967) 48-68 (60f.), who raises the possibility that a *double entendre* may have been intended by the poet.

the far more common of the two verbs *yada*ʿ, "to know".[27] See further below, on *da*ʿ *tô* in v. 11.

53:4   Even if the divine names are used in Hebrew to express the superlative,[28] the phrase *mukkeh* ʾ*elōhîm* can hardly be an example of such an idiom, since it would be pointless for the "we" to say that they "considered" or "esteemed" the servant to be "terribly smitten"[29] when there was no question but that he was (cf. 52:14). The force of vv. 4-5 lies entirely in the contrast between what "we" *believed* was the source of his suffering (God) and what was in fact its source ("our sins"); I have repeated the phrase "by God" with each of the participles in order to emphasise that contrast.[30]

53:7   I have taken *yûbāl* and *ne*ʾ *elāmâ* as the principal verbs of the sentence, since otherwise MT lacks a principal verb (*niggaś* is presumably a participle like *na*ʿ *aneh*[31]). The form *ne*ʾ *elāmâ* need not be emended to *ne*ʾ *elām*;[32] it can be taken as an archaic third person masculine singular (cf. *mal*eʾ *â* ṣ*e*bā ʾ*āh*, 40:2).[33]

53:8   No certainty is attainable in the translation of this problematic verse. I agree with Whybray that its first two words *mē*ʿōṣ*er ûmimmišpāṭ* are best taken in a specific sense, whether of

---

27 The possibility is worth considering that the phrase means "taught by suffering"; for the idea of educative suffering see J. Coste, "Notion grecque et notion biblique de la 'souffrance éducatrice'", *RSR* 43 (1955) 481-522.

28 Cf. D. Winton Thomas, "A Consideration of Some Unusual Ways of Expressing the Superlative in Hebrew", *VT* 3 (1953) 209-24. The word "express" begs the question: it is illegitimate to argue that because Hebrew uses a divine name where we would use the superlative, the divine name means no more than a superlative.

29 Winton Thomas, 123; Whybray, 175, allows that it "perhaps means no more than 'terribly smitten'".

30 Muilenburg, 622, also sees that "by God" is "the crucial phrase that goes with all three words".

31 Of course it is also possible to repoint to *na*ʿ *a nā* (third masc. sing.), in which case *niggaś* would be a niph. perfect.

32 So NAB; see *Textual Notes on the New American Bible* (Paterson, N.J.; St Anthony's Guild, n.d.) 416. NAB, however, does not understand *yûbāl* as a principal verb; it translates "Like a lamb led to the slaughter or a sheep to the shearers, he was silent and opened not his mouth". I prefer to think that *yûbāl* anticipates *luqāḥ* in the next verse.

33 So Dahood, 68.

"arrest" and "trial",[34] or of "prison" and "law-court".[35] Of many other possibilities I mention only those of G.R. Driver, "without protection (of kin) and without due legal procedure"[36] (cf. NEB "without protection, without justice"); M. Dahood, "without restraint and without moderation";[37] P.R. Ackroyd, "from (royal) power and administration";[38] G.W. Ahlström, "from his just position of power";[39] P.A.H. de Boer, "without delay and without judgement";[40] L. Rignell "from a sacred position".[41] As for the term *dôr*, I am inclined to accept the suggestion[42] that the word is cognate with Akk. *dûru(m)* "lasting state", Arab. *dauru(n)* "role (in life)", "turn, time, change (of fortune)" (cf. also Ps. 24:6). Less probable, in my view, is the interpretation of *dôr* as "assembly", "community", hence "royal house" or "dynasty".[43]

For 8a an attractive alternative, in which *dôr* has its usual meaning is offered by the JPS version: "And with his generation who did reason?" (I would prefer: "And against his generation who protested?"). *śîaḥ* with a direct object is attested in Prov. 6:22, where it seems preferable to understand *tᵉśîḥekâ* of the reproving func-

34 Whybray, 176; similarly North, 65, 230ff. ("arrest" and "sentence").

35 Winton Thomas, 124.

36 Driver, 94, comparing *ʿōṣer* with Arab. *ʿaṣîru(n)* "dependent on the family".

37 Dahood, 64,67, taking *ʿōṣer* and *mišpāṭ* as synonymous; but it is doubtful that *ʿōṣer* can have the rather psychological meaning of (self-) restraint (on the part of the servant's persecutors).

38 "The Meaning of Hebrew *dôr* Considered", *JSS* 13 (1968) 3-10 (7); but where else in the poem is it hinted that the servant had any authority or power before his · exaltation by Yahweh?

39 "Notes to Isaiah 53:8f", *BZ* 13 (1969) 95-98 (95ff.), mentioning also several other interpretations not referred to here; the same objection applies to this translation as to the preceding one. Cf. similarly C.C. Torrey: "from dominion and rule he was plucked down" (*The Second Isaiah: a new interpretation* [New York: Scribners, 1928] 419).

40 De Boer, 35. Certainly no emendation of *ʿōṣer* is required, *pace* C.F. Whitley, "Textual Notes on Deutero-Isaiah", *VT* 11 (1961) 457-61 (459f.).

41 Rignell, 82.

42 G.R. Driver, "Linguistic and Textual Problems: Isaiah XL-LXVI", *JTS* 36 (1935) 396-406 (403). Similarly North, 230; Winton Thomas, 124; Whybray, 177.

43 So Ackroyd, "The Meaning of *dôr*" 6f., applying to our passage the suggestion of F.J. Neuberg, "An Unrecognised Meaning of Hebrew *dôr*", *JNES* 9 (1950) 215-17. It is not clear, however, whether Ackroyd understands the text to mean "who considered his royal house (? i.e. the fact that he belonged to a royal house)" or "Who gave a thought to his dynasty, that it was cut off . . .".

tion of wisdom rather than, by transferring the verse to follow 5:19, the "guiding" or "talking" of a loving wife.[44] Improbable is the translation, "Who takes his generation into consideration", i.e. reflects on the significance of this generation of Israel in Yahweh's purposes.[45] On the translation of *śîaḥ* as "protest", see below on chapter 3 d.

The suffix of *ʿammî* is surprising in this context, since in the central three strophes of the poem it is the "we" who speak. There are three possibilities: (i) that *ʿammî* is an abbreviation for *ʿam yhwh*[46] (ii) that we should read *mippiš̌ʿ ām* for *mippešǎʿ ʿammî*;[47] (iii) that we follow the reading of 1QIs[a] *ʿmw*;[48] of these I prefer the last. Less plausible are North's suggestion to read *ʿammê negaʿ lāmô*, lit. "peoples of a striking to them", i.e. "people who deserved to be stricken",[49] and other emendations such as *mippᵉśā̌ ēnû*.[50] On the phrase *negaʿ lāmô*, see below, chapter 2 c (iv).

53:9 The verb *wayyittēn* is either to be taken as an indefinite third person singular[51] or repointed to *wayyuttan*.[52] The translation "criminals" (MT *ʿāšîr* "a rich man") is problematic. None of the usual solutions, whether by emending to *ʿōśê raʿ* "evildoers"[53] or by supposing a second Heb. *ʿāšîr* "rabble" (cognate with Arab.

44 So NAB; NEB; R.B.Y. Scott, *Proverbs, Ecclesiastes* (AB; Garden City, N.Y.: Doubleday, 1965) 55.

45 Rignell, *VT* 3 (1953) 88.

46 See in general G.R. Driver, "Once Again Abbreviations", *Textus* 4 (1964) 76-94 (79).

47 Cf. BH[3].

48 This is possibly also the reading of 1QIs[b]; see K. Elliger, "Nochmals textkritisches zu Jes 53", in *Wort, Lied und Gottesspruch. Festschrift für Joseph Ziegler* (ed. J. Schreiner; Würzburg: Echter, 1972) II, 138. Dahood, 69, believes MT *ʿammî* has a third person suffix, which therefore requires no emendation.

49 North, 230f.

50 As LXX, Syriac, Targum; cf. Elliger, "Nochmals textkritisches" 138ff., who believes that *ʿammî* resulted from an originally defectively written *mippᵉśāʿēmô* "their transgressions".

51 So Driver, 95; Winton Thomas, 124.

52 So Morgenstern, 317.

53 So e.g. Morgenstern, 317.

ĝutrun)[54] is entirely satisfying.[55] Only because some parallel to "wicked" seems needed do I use "criminals". The problem of the imbalance between plural *rᵉšā'îm* "wicked" and singular *ʿāšîr* "rich" is eased by Dahood's examples of parallels between singular and plural (Is. 52:14 [in this very poem]: *'îš//bᵉnê 'ādām*; Jb. 20:5; Prov. 14:33),[56] but the meaning is still obscure: one can imagine criminals' being buried in a place apart, and the rich having their own burial spots, but would they be the same place? There can at least be little doubt that the last word of 9a is to be read *bāmūtô* or *bômātô* "his burial mound" (cf. 1QIsᵃ *bwmtw*).[57]

"Non-violence" is perhaps the best translation of the compound noun *lō' - ḥāmās*; it is not said *lō' ʿāśâ ḥāmās*. The conjunction *ʿal* (for *ʿal 'ᵃšer*), though universally translated "although" by modern commentators,[58] elsewhere means "because", and should perhaps be taken in an ironic sense here (the only support for the translation "although" comes from a verbally similar passage, Job 16:17, which may be similarly understood).

53:10   I take the controverted *heḥᵉlî* as an infinitive absolute (read *haḥᵃley*, and normally spelled *haḥᵃleh*) of *ḥlh* "be sick".[59] Other interpretations are, however, possible and attractive: (i) *heḥᵉlîm 'et-śām 'ăšām napšô* "he healed the one who made himself a sacrifice for sin";[60] but *'et-* with an anarthrous participle is

---

54 So A. Guillaume, "A Contribution to Hebrew Lexicography", *BSOAS* 16 (1954) 1-12 (10); followed by Driver, 95, and NEB "the refuse of mankind".

55 Still less the view that *ʿšyr* is essentially a word-play on *ršym* and that "the original meaning of *ʿšyr* is perhaps of secondary importance" (Ahlström, "Notes" 97f.).

56 Dahood, 70; North, 231, and de Boer, 114, take *ʿāšîr* as a collective.

57 As proposed by W.F. Albright, "The High Place in Ancient Palestine", *VTSup* 4 (1957) 242-58 (244ff.); see too S. Iwry, "*Maṣṣēbāh and bāmāh* in 1Q Isaiahᴬ 6:13", *JBL* 76 (1957) 225-32 (232); Albright is followed by Winton Thomas, 125; cf. Driver, 95f.

58 Some medieval Jewish commentators, however, attempted to take *ʿal* in its usual sense. So Rashi commented: "he gave himself up to any form of death which had been decreed upon him, *because* he would not deny God by perpetrating violence and doing evil like all the nations"; and ibn Ezra: "like Samson . . . they [the exiles] desired to die with the nations amongst whom they dwelt . . . And that this desire arose indeed from their distress is shewn by what follows, *because he did no violence*" (S.R. Driver and A. Neubauer, *The Fifty-Third Chapter of Isaiah according to the Jewish Interpreters* [1877; r.p. New York: Ktav, 1969] II, 38f., 47).

59 Following Winton Thomas, 125.

60 So Begrich, 64; followed by Driver, 96f.; cf. NEB.

rather rare; (ii) *wᵉhû šām ʾāšām napšō* "and he (the servant) made his life a sin-offering";[61] I would prefer, however, to take *wᵉhû*ʾ as referring to Yahweh: "and it was he who made his (the servant's) life a sin-offering". Less convincing emendations are offered by H.L. Ginsberg, who finds another reference here to Yahweh's arm,[62] by I. Sonne, who posits a large-scale misplacement of lines,[63] by H.P. Müller who offers several emendations of vv. 10-11[64] and by J. Coppens, who finds here the Deutero-Isaianic qualities of the ideal king, *yirʾâ* and *daʿat*, reads *wᵉdaʿat* for MT *bᵉdaʿto* (1QIsᵃ *wbdʿtw* could have been used as support), and translates "de crainte il sera comblé et de connaissance".[65] The difficult *tāśîm* may be read as *tuśam*,[66] emended to *yāśîm*,[67] or perhaps preferably, allowed to stand, with *napšô* its subject.[68] The noun *ḥēpeṣ* is used, I assume, in its late sense of "business", hence "plans" (cf. Ec. 3:1; 1QS 3.17).

53:11 Any interpretation can only be tentative; the translation above assumes that (i) *yirʾeh* is an orthographic variant for *yirweh* < *rwh* "be saturated, drink one's fill" (cf. Ps. 60:5; 91:16);[69] (ii) *daʿtô* is here from *ydʿ* II "to be submissive, humiliated", and so parallel to *ʿᵃmal-napšô*;[70] (iii) *yaṣdîq* is an internal *hiphʿil*,

61 K. Elliger, "Jes 53:10: alte crux - neuer Vorschlag", *MIO* (R. Meyer Festschrift) 15 (1969) 228-33; anticipated by E. Kutsch, *Sein Leiden und Tod - unser Heil* (Neukirchen: Neukirchener Verlag des Erziehungsvereins, 1967), 30ff. (see Elliger, "Nochmals textkritisches" 137).

62 Ginsberg, "The Arm of Yhwh" 156.

63 "Isaiah 53:10-12", *JBL* 78 (1959) 335-42.

64 "Ein Vorschlag zu Jes 53:10f.", *ZAW* 81 (1969) 377-80.

65 "La finale du quatrième Chant du Serviteur (Is., LIII, 10-12)", *ETL* 39 (1963) 114-19 (118).

66 Torrey, *Second Isaiah, in loc.*; cf. Driver, "Problems: Isaiah XL-LXVI" 403 (*tûśam*); and BHS ("prp *tuśam*").

67 E.g. Cheyne, 93; similarly RSV.

68 Muilenburg, 628; North, 232. This is the traditional Jewish interpretation.

69 See Winton Thomas, 125f.; Driver, 97f.

70 See above on 53:3. B. Reicke, without referring to the postulated *ydʿ* II, reached the similar conclusion, that "knowledge" here means obedience or submission: "The Knowledge of the Suffering Servant", in *Das ferne und nahe Wort. Festschrift Leonhard Rost* (ed. F. Maass; BZAW 103; Berlin: Töpelmann, 1967) 186-92.

"showed himself righteous", [71] i.e. was proved righteous; (iv) *'abdî* is either an abbreviation for *'ebed yhwh*, [72] an orthographic variant of *'abdò*, [73] or, most probably, a scribal error for *'abdô*. [74]

53:12 I accept the view of Driver that confusion in the MT between *ḥlq* qal and *ḥlq* pi' el allows us to repoint *y^{e}ḥallēq* "he shall allot a share" as *yaḥ^{a}lōq* "he shall receive a share". [75] I also take *bārabbîm* as "*among* the great" and *'et-'^{a}ṣûmîm* as "*with* the strong", but it is also possible to take each as the object of its respective verb: "I give him the mighty as his portion, and the powerful he divides as spoil". [76] It remains uncertain whether the *rabbîm* in vv. 11,12 are the "great ones" or "the many", whether the presence of the article makes any difference, and whether the same group is in view in both these verses. I incline to regard *hārabbîm* (vv. 11,12) as equivalent to the *m^{e}lākîm* of 52:15, and *rabbîm* as the equivalent of *rabbîm* in 52:14 and *gōyim rabbîm* in 52:15. [77] On *he$^{'e}$râ lammāwet*, see below, chapter 2 c (i). The verb *nimnâ* is probably a *niph'al tolerativum*. [78]

71 S. Mowinckel, followed by Whybray, 181. Westermann, 267, approves Mowinckel's view, but translates "shall justify many" (p. 255, cf. p. 256 "effect righteousness for many").

72 See note 46 above. Duhm, 393, had already suggested that *'bdy* in this poem was an abbreviation for *'bd yhwh*.

73 Dahood, 72.

74 For a different interpretation, supplying the objects *yiś'î* and *tôb* to the verbs *yir'eh* and *yiśbā'*, see G. Schwarz, "»... sieht er ... wird er satt ...«?", *ZAW* 84 (1972) 356-58. See also the study of I. Blythin, "A Consideration of Difficulties in the Hebrew Text of Isaiah 53:11", *Bible Translator* 17 (1966) 27-31.

75 Driver, 102.

76 Cf. Winton Thomas, 120; Coppens, "La finale" 115; Muilenburg, 631.

77 For a discussion see Coppens, "La finale" 114ff. A similar problem occurs in Qumran texts; cf. J. Carmignac, "HRYBYM: les «Nombreux» ou les «Notables»?", *R de Q* 7 (1969-71) 575-86. J. Morgenstern hazards the idea that the *rabbîm* here may be the members of a sect, as they are at Qumran, and is certainly inclined to delete the article from *hārabbîm* and *bārabbîm* (53:11f.): "Two Additional Notes to 'The Suffering Servant - a New Solution'", *VT* 13 (1963) 321-32 (331f.).

78 GKC§51c; Winton Thomas, 126; Whybray, 182; Westermann, 268f.

2.   THE UNSAID : ENIGMA AND AMBIGUITY

2.   The unsaid : enigma and ambiguity

Isaiah 53 has become a casualty of historical-critical scholarship. It is not the only Biblical text in that plight, but its injuries are more grave than those of many others. Historical-critical scholarship is bound to mistreat a cryptic poetic text when it regards it as a puzzle to be solved, a code to be cracked. What if the force of the poem - to say nothing of the poetry of the poem - lies in its very unforthcomingness, its refusal to be precise and to give *information*, its stubborn concealment of the kind of data that critical scholarship yearns to get its hands on as the building-blocks for the construction of its hypotheses?

The enigmas of Isaiah 53 are too well recognized to need a detailed rehearsal here. But it is crucial for this study to confront their range and complexity afresh.

a.   Who is "he"?

The problem of Deutero-Isaianic studies has long been the identity of the servant of Yahweh: "Of whom speaketh the prophet thus?" (Ac. 8:34, in reference to Isa. 53:7-8). C.R. North in his study of this question recounts the despair of a commentator of a previous generation who "abandoned his projected commentary on Isaiah because this part of his subject overwhelmed him".[1] By 1948, however, when North's work was first published, it could be asserted with some confidence that only four identifications of the servant commanded serious support:

i   An anonymous contemporary of Second Isaiah
ii   Second Isaiah himself
iii   A group (whether all Israel, ideal Israel, a remnant, or the prophets)
iv   The expected Davidic messiah.

This is not the place to elaborate a current *status quaestionis* or compile a catalogue of further identification. Yet the following impressionistic survey will serve to highlight the intractability of our question. The view that the servant is the prophet himself, though much out of favour in recent decades, has latterly been

---

1 C.R. North, *The Suffering Servant in Deutero-Isaiah. An Historical and Critical Study* (London: Oxford University Press, 2nd edn., 1956) 1. The reference is to S.R. Driver.

championed again by the latest commentary in English, that of R.N. Whybray.[2] H.M. Orlinsky has found the servant of 52:13 (Israel) to be different from the servant of 53:11 (the prophet).[3] New twists to the collective interpretation are given by N.H. Snaith, who finds the servant of Yahweh in "the first batch of exiles, those who went into captivity with the young king Jehoiachin in 597 B.C., together with a tendency to include also the 586 B.C. exiles",[4] and by D.N. Freedman, who finds the servant in eschatological Israel.[5]

In several other recent writers the collective and individual interpretations merge. According to O. Kaiser, the servant is both the exiled people and the prophet himself who represents Israel in its prophetic role.[6] A.S. Kapelrud agrees that the servant is exiled Israel, but since the king is the "real representative" of the people, "it is one and the same thing to say that the Servant of Yahweh was the suffering and exiled people or that he was the suffering and exiled king",Jehoiachin.[7] W.M.W. Roth has argued that the servant is the ideal or typical prophet, and so portrays "the prophetic office in its direct and superior relationship to Yahweh".[8] The most recent paper on the subject makes yet another proposal, that the servant is the city of Zion as cult centre and symbol of Israel.[9]

No further comment is needed to underscore the enigmatic

2 Whybray, 71, 171f.

3 Orlinsky, 17-23.

4 Snaith, 170.

5 D.N. Freedman, "The Slave of Yahweh", *Western Watch* 10 (1959) 1-9, known to me only from the discussion of his view by A.O. Schwartzentruber, *The Servant Songs in Relation to their Context in Deutero-Isaiah: A Critique of Contemporary Methodologies* (Princeton Dissertation, 1970; Xerox University Microfilms, Ann Arbor, Michigan, 1975) 18-46.

6 O. Kaiser, *Der königliche Knecht: eine traditionsgeschichtlich-exegetische Studie über die Ebed-Jahwe-Lieder bei Deuterojesaja* (FRLANT, N.F. 52; Göttingen: Vandenhoeck und Ruprecht, 1959) 65, 132.

7 A.S. Kapelrud, "The Identity of the Suffering Servant", in *Near Eastern Studies in Honor of William Foxwell Albright* (ed. H. Goedicke; Baltimore: Johns Hopkins Press, 1971), 307-14 (313).

8 W.M.W. Roth, "The Anonymity of the Suffering Servant", *JBL* 83 (1964) 171-79 (179).

9 L.E. Wilshire, "The Servant-City: A New Interpretation of the 'Servant of the Lord' in the Servant Songs of Deutero-Isaiah", *JBL* 94 (1975) 356-67.

nature of literature that permits such a multiplicity of interpretation.

b.   What did "he" suffer?

The servant is of stunted growth (53:2), physically unattractive (53:2), ostracised by men (53:3), suffering pain in general (53:3) and particular physical injury or disease (53:4f.); in addition he is subjected to some quasi-judicial punishment (53:7-9), which results in his being "cut off out of the land of the living" (53:8). To what extent this language depicts the biographical details of the servant's life, and to what extent it is the traditional language of suffering employed in the Psalms is a matter of dispute.

Some observe that "it is difficult to pinpoint any statement in the Song which unequivocally refers to natural sickness",[10] others that suffering in silence at the hand of aggressors is a traditional psalmic theme (cf. Ps. 38:14-15 [EVV 13-14])[11] Most would agree with J. Muilenburg that "the wide diversity of terms used to describe the suffering . . . forbid[s] any attempt to identify its precise nature",[12] and with C. Westermann that of the two typical modes of suffering referred to in the poem "there is no reason for taking either the one (illness, e.g. leprosy) or the other (violence or conviction) as a literal, true to life description".[13]

c.   Did "he" die?

Not even a question so apparently crucial for an interpretation of the poem as this, "Did the servant actually die?", admits of a clear answer. The majority view has consistently been in the affirmative, in spite of dissension by E. Sellin and W. Staerk who at one stage regarded the servant as Jehoiachin.[14] But in recent years

---

10 Payne, 134.

11 Whybray, 176.

12 Muilenburg, 622. Cf. Wade, 341: "The language is rhetorical and not meant to be understood literally". (This is with particular reference to 53:7, but the commentator plainly regards all the allusions to [Israel's] suffering as figurative.)

13 Westermann, 265.

14 See North, *Suffering Servant* 148.

H.M. Orlinsky,[15] G.R. Driver,[16] R.N. Whybray,[17] and J.A. Soggin[18] have declared themselves unconvinced; and the weight of their names ensures that this question too must now be ranked among the enigmas of Isaiah 53.

The expressions in the poem which do indeed suggest death are not necessarily to be taken in that sense:

(i) In 53:12 $he^{ce}r\hat{a}$ $lamm\bar{a}wet$ $naps\check{o}$ (RSV "he poured out his soul to death") might well mean "he exposed his life to (the danger of) death".[19]

(ii) In 53:9 $wayitt\bar{e}n^{20}$ $'et-r^{ev}\check{s}\bar{a}^{c}\hat{i}m$ $qibr\hat{o}$ (RSV "they made his grave with the wicked") again does not imply the servant's actual death. The preparation of a sufferer's grave by his enemies in anticipation of his imminent death is a literary stereotype, attested also in *Ludlul bēl nēmeqi*: "My grave was waiting, and my funerary paraphernalia ready; before I was in fact dead, the funeral lament was set up over me; my whole land said: How has he been brought to nothing!"[21]

(iii) In 53:8 $nigzar$ $m\bar{e}'$ $ere\d{s}$ $\d{h}ayy\hat{i}m$ (RSV "He was cut off out of the land of the living"), J.A. Soggin has recently demonstrated that this expression "relates to the hopeless situation in the individual laments when it is said that a man has fallen into the hands of death".[22]

(iv) In 53:8 many commentators and versions adopt the emen-

15 Orlinsky, 60f.

16 Driver, 104f.

17 Whybray, 171f., 177f.

18 J.A. Soggin, "Tod und Auferstehung des leidenden Gottesknechtes Jesaja 53. 8-10", *ZAW* 87 (1975) 346-55.

19 So Whybray, 182; Driver, 102; Orlinsky, 62. The verb $he^{ce}r\hat{u}$, hiph'il of $^{c}ar\hat{a}$ "be naked, bare", is as likely to mean "made bare" as "poured out" (cf. $^{c}ar\hat{a}$ in Gen. 24:20, of emptying a water pot), especially if $nepe\check{s}$ here has any overtone of the meaning "neck, throat" (cf. Ps. 105:18; Job 14:2; Prov. 22:25). It is unnecessary to argue that $m\bar{a}wet$ here has simply a superlative force, viz. "he gave himself to the uttermost" (Winton Thomas, 120, 126; similarly Driver, 102f.).

20 Usually emended to $wayyuttan$ or $wayyitt^{e}n\hat{u}$.

21 W.G. Lambert, *Babylonian Wisdom Literature* (Oxford: Clarendon Press, 1960) 46.

22 Soggin, "Tod und Auferstehung" 354; for the opposite view, see e.g. Payne, 138; for the view that $nigzar$ stands for $nigraz$ "disappeared from", see L. Delekat, "Zum hebräischen Wörterbuch", *VT* 14 (1964) 7-66 (13).

dation of *nega' lāmô* "there was a blow to him (? to them)"[23] to *nugga' lammāwet* "he was smitten to death" in accord with LXX *ēchthē eis thanaton*. Needless to say, the emendation is unnecessary,[24] the LXX reading proves nothing about the Hebrew text,[25] and even if *lammāwet* is original, it could always be argued that "to death" is only an idiom for "grievously".[26]

In none of these cases is it my intention to argue that the poem does *not* speak of the servant's death, although the scholars cited above have argued vigorously that it does not. It is enough for my purpose - rather, it is precisely my point - to observe that the references to the servant's "death" are all ambiguous,[27] and to add this item also to my list of enigmas in Isaiah 53.

d.   Who are "we"?

Here the range of options is more limited, but the cryptic character of the poem is equally evident. Are the "we" who have heard the report about the servant (53:1), who once regarded him as "of no account", but have now come to see that "they were our sufferings that weighed on him" (53:4), the prophet and like-minded Israelites, the prophet's disciples, Israel as a whole, or the "peoples" and "kings" of 52:15?

On one side, there seems to be a smooth transition from 52:15 to 53:1 : in 52:15 peoples and kings "see" and "ponder" a sight they have never seen before and a message never heard before, while in 53:1 "we" remark on how incredible is what "we" have heard and what has been seen.[28] From another perspective, it can

---

23 See GKC §103f (p. 302 n. 3).

24 *Pace* Driver, 95, who finds *nega' lāmô* "not possible"; the emendation is also supported by the careful study of Elliger, "Nochmals textkritisches" 138ff.

25 The LXX clearly understood the servant to have died and may consequently have read a Hebrew *lmw* as an abbreviation for *lmwt* (cf. Winton Thomas, 124 n. 34; Driver, 95; *id.*, "Abbreviations", 94).

26 So Driver, 95; Winton Thomas, 124.

27 As Driver says, "No phrase is used which unambiguously implies his death" (p. 104).

28 So Westermann, 260: "The transition from divine utterance to report is scarcely noticeable. The introduction (v.1) . . . takes up [the] final words [of 52:15], repeating that what is now to be related has never before been heard of, and doing this now from the standpoint of those who learned of the change (vv. 14f.)". Similarly Marti, 356; Morgenstern, 298, 314.

be argued that "the heathen could not possibly give expression to thoughts so deep that they have no parallel in the OT . . . The interpretation of the Servant's sufferings must be the Prophet's".[29] Yet there is nothing to prevent the prophet's putting his own interpretation of the servant upon the lips of the "nations": a poet can use various "speaking voices" to give expression to his vision.[30] It would be more persuasive to argue that the $\check{s}^e m\hat{u}\,{}^c\hat{a}$ of 53:1 is properly a prophetic audition,[31] and that the "conversion" of the "we" to recognize God's purpose in the suffering of the servant corresponds well with the "conversion" of the prophet himself in the call-narrative of 40:6-8.[32] To similar effect J. Skinner claimed that the "we" must be the Israelites, "or one Israelite (perhaps the prophet himself) speaking in the name of all", since: (i) in 52:15 the Gentiles are surprised at the servant's exaltation because they had not previously heard of it, whereas in 53:1 "we" *have* heard of it; (ii) the Gentiles revise their opinion of the servant because of his ultimate exaltation (52:14f.), whereas in Isa. 53 the "we" have already changed their view of the servant and his exaltation is regarded as yet to occur; (iii) the expression "my people" in 53:8 can only make sense on the lips of an Israelite.[33]

Of course every such argument can be countered, and fresh support for the equation of "we" with the nations can be adduced, especially if the poem is interpreted in the context of the other so-called "Servant Songs", where the poet himself does not speak, and the scope of the servant's mission apparently reaches beyond the confines of Israel - which would not be the case here if all the nations do is stand and gape at the servant (52:14f.).[34]

29 North, 236.

30 Cf. W.F. Lanahan, "The Speaking Voice in the Book of Lamentations", *JBL* 93 (1974) 41-49 (41): "The *persona* is not to be thought of as a fiction. It is a creative procedure in the displacement of the poet's imagination beyond the limitations of his single viewpoint so that he may gain a manifold insight into the human experience . . . The use of [a] *persona* by the poet enriches his intuition."

31 So Duhm, 395, adding, "Warum soll es nicht der Dichter sein, da doch mit keiner Silbe auf so fernstehende Subjekte hingewiesen wird?".

32 Following the interpretation of 40:6-8 set out by Westermann, 41, "When he demurs with his counter-cry, 'What shall I preach?', he is only 'one of the people', and he speaks as one whose own thoughts are those of the vanquished nation that no longer believes in the possibility of any new beginning".

33 Skinner, 136f. The "we" are identified with Israel also by McKenzie, 133f.

34 Cf. Whitehouse, 199.

Yet another possibility is offered by R.N. Whybray: the "we" are Second Isaiah's disciples,[35] who compose Isa. 53 as a psalm of thanksgiving for the deliverance of the prophet from trouble, possibly his release from a Babylonian prison; the form of the poem is that of the individual thanksgiving, "with the unusual feature that it is not the former sufferer himself but his friends who give thanks".[36] These disciples, it should be noted, "identify themselves with the whole community" in their confession, "all we like sheep had gone astray" (53:6).[37]

e.   **What led the "we" to change their minds about the Servant?**

C. Westermann rightly points out that this is a question that goes deeper than "Who is he?", and comments that it is a question as little resolved as the other. The actual way in which the "we" came to change their minds about the servant, Westermann says, "remains secret. And where the report is silent we must defer to it".[38]

f.   **Who are "they"?**

Intricately bound up with the question of the "we" is this of the identity of the "they", the persons spoken of in the third person. What is the connection between the "they" of 52:14-15, the "many" *(rabbîm)*, the "many *or* great nations", and the "kings", who view the elevation of the humiliated servant with amazement, and the "they" of 53:11-12, the "many" *(hārabbîm)* before whom the servant is proved righteous (*or*, to whom the servant brings salvation) and whose punishment *(ᶜāwôn)* he bears, the "many" or the "great ones" *(hārabbîm)* with whom he shares the spoil, the "rebels" *(pōsᵉᶜîm)* with whom he is counted, and the "many" *(rabbîm)* whose punishment *(ḥēṭ')* he bears?

Are the "they" in both cases the same group? If so, are they the

35 Cf. P.-E. Dion. "L'universalisme religieux dans les différentes couches redactionalles d'Isaïe 4–55", Bib 51 (1970) 161-82 (177): "un choeur de Juifs devenus les disciples du Serviteur souffrant".

36 Whybray, 172.

37 Whybray, 176.

38 Westermann, 264f.

Gentiles, "the efficacy of the Servant's work [being] confessed by all who were included in the scope of his mission, i.e. the Gentiles (xlii. 1-4, xlix. 1-6), otherwise they are left at the end as mere spectators with nothing to say . . . Their dumb astonishment . . . might be temporary, to be followed by voluble speech".[39] Or are they in both cases Jews, the Jews of the diaspora being spoken of as "nations" because they are far distant from the events described and as "kings" because some of them move in exalted circles?[40] Or, to put it slightly differently, are they "crypto-Israelites" who have merged their identity with the nations of the dispersion but who come to recognize in the suffering Israel of Babylonian exile their true identity?[41]

Or, is it that the "they" comprise two quite different groups? J.L. McKenzie, for example, sees the "many" of 52:14 as Israelites, the "nations" and "kings" of 52:15 as Gentiles, and the "they" of ch. 53 as Israelites, fellows of the innocent Israelite who suffers on their behalf.[42] For R.N. Whybray, the "they" of 52:14f. are Gentiles, as are also the *rabbîm* of 53:12a, whereas elsewhere in ch. 53 the "they" are Israelites because of whom and in common with whom the Servant suffered.[43] Others, like P.A.H. de Boer,[44] take it for granted that Gentiles are in view in 52:14f., and Israelites only in ch. 53.

Or can it be that the "they" include throughout the poem both Jews and Gentiles? L. Rignell remarks that the expiation (as he understands it) of 52:15a "primarily affects Israel as a whole, and secondly the Gentiles. Both these groups are surely represented in the expression 'many people' *(gwym rbym)*"; and on 53:11 he comments that the "many" "refers above all to the children of Israel but may also have a wider meaning and refer to the Gen-

39 North, 236.

40 Westermann, 259. He continues: "Deutero-Isaiah is thinking of the widespread publicity to be given to the work, but not of heathen spheres outside Israel".

41 Cf. D.E. Hollenberg, "Nationalism and 'the nations' in Isaiah XL-LV" *VT* 19 (1969) 23-36 (35f.).

42 McKenzie, 132, 134.

43 Whybray, 170, 182f.

44 De Boer, 112f., 115f.

tiles".[45]

It is not my purpose here to attempt to decide this issue; it is rather to point to the ambiguity of the poem, and in so doing to suggest that it is of its essence that unequivocal identifications are not made[46] and that the poem in this respect also is open-ended and allows for multiple interpretations.[47]

45 Rignell, 79,84. Cf. Fohrer, 162: "muss man die nicht völlig eindeutige Ausdrücksweise in Kauf nehmen und manchmal in das von einer Gruppe Gesagte die andere Gruppe einschliessen". Hollenberg has also pointed to the overlap between the two groups, Israel and the nations, though he has not applied his observation to ch. 53 ("Nationalism" 28f., 34ff.).

46 I assume, though the poem itself barely entitles me to, that the "I" is Yahweh; but even this assumption that Yahweh speaks in the poem has not gone unchallenged: Duhm regarded the first person indicators of 52:13; 53:11,12 as "easily eliminated" (p. 393).

47 Muilenberg, 631, is reaching toward a similar conclusion when he comments of the poem as a whole: "all Israel [i.e. including the Christian church] - in its varying distances and guises, held succinct and understood in its maximum form as a person - is present".

3.   HOW SAID : RHETORIC

3.   How said : rhetoric

Rhetorical criticism, as has been amply attested in recent years, is not a mechanical matter of identifying stylistic devices, but, on the premise of the unity of form and content of a work of art, moves towards the work's meaning and quiddity from the standpoint of form rather than of content, of the "how said" rather than the "what said". The concentration is upon the text in itself, that is, in the first place, irrespective of its context. In the end, of course, understanding of the work will develop fully only when text and context are brought into relationship – a relationship of dialogue or mutual illumination, that is the hermeneutical circle as Schleiermacher conceived it,[1] in which the parts make sense only in terms of the whole and vice versa. But in order for that dialogue to begin, the identity of the two partners to it - text and context - has to be recognized and respected. Historical-critical scholarship has tended to approach the individual unit of Biblical literature (the "text") from the standpoint of its context, whether that be its frame of reference (as in *Einleitungswissenschaft*) or of its generic affinities (as in *Formgeschichte*). The present section is an attempt to redress that imbalance by focussing on the text in itself.[2]

a.   Personae

Most impressive in this poem is the function of the four *personae* – "I", "he", "we", and "they". The movement of the poem is wholly occupied by them and by the various connections among them. While matters of time and place are absent from view altogether, and questions of identity are out of focus - to say the least - the nexus of relationships among the four *personae* is perspicuous, and obviously at the heart of the poem's significance. That only pronouns are regularly employed for the *dramatis personae* of the poem evidences its potency.[3]

The "I" is related to the "he" in these ways:

---

1   Cf. R.E. Palmer, *Hermeneutics. Interpretation Theory in Schleiermacher, Dilthey, Heidegger, and Gadamer* (Evanston: Northwestern University Press, 1969) 87f.

2   For that reason I cannot agree with de Boer, 110, that "an attempt to understand the meaning of the passage in agreement with its context seems to me our first task".

3   Cf. Muilenburg, 624.

1. The "I" presents "him" (52:13) for admiration as his servant.
2. The "I" announces "his" supremacy (52:13).
3. The "I" reports on the attitude of "them" to "him" (52:15).
4. "He" was *only wrongly* thought to be struck down by the "I" (53:4).
5. The "I" laid suffering on him (53:6,10).
6. The "I" allots him a portion with the great (53:12).

There is a dual aspect to the relationship of "I" and "he". For the most part, the "I" supports the "he", but the "I" also allows "him" to grow up stunted and lays suffering on him. This is not an ambiguity as far as the poem is concerned or a tension that needs to be resolved: these are the true facts of the matter.

In the relationship "we" - "he", however, two opposite attitudes are expressed, the latter cancelling out the former. Here the duality is contrastive, and resolution comes about through the elimination of the first pole of the duality: the attitude of the "we" to "him" *changes* from hostility or scorn to appreciation. The duality is particularly marked in strophe 3.

The relationship "he" - "they" is less sharply defined, but here also there is a duality. If we are correct in identifying the "they" of 52:14f. (the *gōyîm rabbîm* and *mᵉlākîm*) with the "they" of 53:12 (*hārabbîm* and *ᶜaṣûmîm*)[4] and probably also with *hārabbîm* of 53:11, there is again a contrastive duality, of non-involvement and involvement. In 52:14f. the "they" merely look at him, shut their mouths in astonishment at him, and ponder what they have heard *about* him - that is, he is an object to them. In 53:11f. they are involved *with* him in that he joins their ranks and shares booty with them (53:12a), he is proved innocent (*yaṣdîq*) in their sight, i.e. to their satisfaction, and he "bears" their guilt (*ᶜāwôn*, 11b) by suffering in intervention (*hipgîaᶜ*) for them (53:12). Here the duality is resolved through harmonisation of its two poles: their objectified contemplation of him (52:14f.) is not negated by their involvement with him, but caught up in it.

The most significant element in this *persona*-analysis is that the "he" stands in the centre of the nexus of relationships. That is, of the six relationships theoretically possible among the four *person-*

4 And perhaps with *hārabbîm* of 53:11.

ae, only three are strong, and the other three barely exist. Diagrammatically:

The poem is almost entirely taken up with the relationships in which "he" figures.[5] Even though, from the point of view of structure, an "I" speech begins and ends the poem, the central figure is plainly the "he". And even though it is said in 53:6b that the suffering of the servant — which is the central event of the poem — has been brought about by the one who speaks as "I", again it is "his" suffering, and not primarily his being made to suffer, that is the poem's concern.

As for the other relationships: that of the "I" and the "they" is non-existent (except perhaps through the intervention of·"him"; cf. 53:12b); that of the "we" and the "they" is so opaque that it qualifies, as we have seen above, as one of the enigmas of the poem; and that of the "I" and the "we" is nowhere explicit, though the "we" recognise a relationship with the "I" through "him" (53:6b).

In *persona* analysis we may also look at the relationships of the *personae* from the point of view of *number*. Here there is a marked pattern: on the one side are the two plural groups: "we" and

5 Cf. Muilenburg's remark that the servant is "intensely present though never named" (p. 615).

"they". The singular persons are from the beginning in strong relationship: "he" is "my" servant (52:13), "he" is the one in whom God's power is revealed (53:1), it is the "I" who causes "him" to suffer (53:6,10), "he" is again "my" servant (53:11), and the "I" assigns a portion to "him" (53:12). The plural groups do not at first appear to have any relationship - there is no verbal link between them. But they have one thing in common: their attitude of disgust towards the servant. As the poem proceeds their attitude changes: that on the part of the "we", from rejection to acceptance, is strongly marked, while on the part of the "they" it is more distantly hinted that "he" becomes accepted by "them" in that he participates *with* them (*bārabbîm, 'et-ʿᵃṣûmîm*, 53:12). Finally the identity of the "we" and the "they" virtually merges as "he" is shown to have the same relationship to both groups: that is, "he" bears (*nāśāʾ, sābal*) the sufferings and pains of the "we" (53:4), and also bears (*sābal, nāśāʾ*) the guilt (*ʿāwôn*) and sin (*ḥēṭʾ*) of the "they", the *rabbîm* (53:11b, 12b).

b. **Visual analysis**

The poem is rich in the language of seeing. That is only to be expected since it is concerned with how to see, i.e. how the servant should be seen.

If we trace first the use of explicitly visual language, we can note the initial "Behold", *hinnēh* (52:13), which already announces that this poem is about "seeing" - seeing the servant of Yahweh, that is; in what way he should and should not be seen. We next meet with how the servant *is* seen initially, with his disfigured appearance (*marʾēhû*, 52:14); that is an external, physical, seeing. Then comes a seeing which is partly physical but partly also an intellectual "seeing": "what had not previously been recounted to them they see (*rāʾû*)" (52:15b). That cannot mean that they have just now seen the most disfigured person of all time, but they have had brought to their attention that this person of disfigured appearance (*marʾēhû*) to whom their attention is drawn (*hinnēh*) is in fact the servant of Yahweh (*ʿabdî*, 52:13). They do not believe it, they do not even understand it, but they are brought to contemplate it (*rāʾû*); therefore the appropriate parallel verb is *hitbōnānû* "they ponder".

40

The reaction of the "we" to the servant is also expressed in highly visual language. He had no "form" ($t\bar{o}^{\,a}ar$) or "splendour" ($h\bar{a}d\bar{a}r$) to make "us" "regard" him ($w^e nir^{\,}\bar{e}h\hat{u}$)[6] and no "appearance" ($mar\,'eh$) that "we" should desire him. The "we" are those from whom he must withdraw his disfigured appearance ($k^e mast\bar{e}r$ [read $k^e mastir$] $p\bar{a}n\hat{i}m\ mimmenn\hat{u}$, 53:3).[7]

"Seeing" for the "we" and the "they" is a symbol of their attitude to the servant; for him, however, seeing symbolises his future and the fruitfulness of his suffering. So he, after his suffering "sees" ($yir\,'eh$) seed (53:10), and, perhaps, if the translation given above is incorrect, after (or, "out of" $[min]$) his life's labour "sees" ($yir\,'eh$)[8] to the point of satiation ($yi\acute{s}b\bar{a}^{\,c}$, 53:11).

There is also less explicitly visual language in the poem. The elevation of the servant ($y\bar{a}r\hat{u}m\ w^e ni\acute{s}\acute{s}\bar{a}'w^e g\bar{a}bah\ m^{e\,'}\bar{o}d$, 52:13), introduced by $hinn\bar{e}h$, is obviously some visible act of exaltation. The "revealing" ($nigl\bar{a}t\hat{a}$, 53:1) of God's arm in the history of the servant similarly points to a visual experience. And since $r\bar{a}\,'\hat{a}$, "to see", in this poem signifies "consider" as well, the expressions of "reckoning" ($l\bar{o}\,'\ h^a \check{s}abnuh\hat{u}$, 53:3; $h^a \check{s}abnuh\hat{u}$, 53:4) may also belong here.

This then is a poem about modes of seeing the servant.

c. Act/agent analysis

Here we have to consider: what is done in the poem, by whom, and to whom?

The overwhelming impression is that most of the action in the poem is done by or to the servant. He is the primary agent and the one most acted upon. The verbal usage confirms this impression. A necessarily imprecise[9] count of verbs and participles in the poem reaches a total of 61, of which 39 refer to the servant, 5 to the "they", 6 to "we", 4 to "Yahweh" and 7 to other subjects which are not *personae* of the poem.

6 If that reading is correct.

7 Or, following RSV, etc., the "we" can only avert their gaze from him.

8 I am not persuaded that $\,'\bar{o}r$ "light" should be inserted as the object of $yir\,'eh$, following LXX and 1QIs^a, though it would not affect the argument if it were; see chapter 1 above for comment on the text.

9 Some textual uncertainties make precision impossible.

The servant appears to be acted upon as much as he acts: while he is the subject of 21 active verbs, he is the subject of 18 passive verbs. But that statistic is misleading. For among the (grammatically) "active" verbs of which he is the subject are a number which do not involve activity on his part: he "did not open his mouth", he "bore", he "carried", he "is high", he "prolongs his days". If we ask, What in fact does the servant do, as distinct from having done to him?, the answer is: very little. He grew up, he did non-violence, (perhaps) he makes himself a sin-offering ($'\bar{a}\check{s}\bar{a}m$), (perhaps) he brings salvation ($ya\d{s}d\hat{i}q$),[10] he takes a share of the booty,[11] he exposes himself to death, he "intervened" ($yapg\hat{i}a^c$, 53:12) - whatever that means[12] - for transgressors.

In other words, there is *no concrete action* that the servant does - apart from letting everything happen to him. Even when it is said, "By him Yahweh's plans ($\d{h}\bar{e}pe\d{s}$) prosper" (53:10), nothing in the way of action on the servant's part can be meant apart from what has been meant throughout the entire poem: Yahweh's purpose was ($\d{h}\bar{a}pe\d{s}$, 53:10) that the servant should - not *do* something - but suffer, be the one acted upon.

d.   Speech analysis

To highlight the significance of this analysis, it may be of value to refer to a report on a structuralist study by Roland Barthes. Barthes, in discussing Acts 10:1 - 11:18, notes that the principal action of the *personae* (the angel, Cornelius, the members of Cornelius' household, Peter, the church at Jerusalem) is *to speak*. From this observation he is able to conclude - though naturally other factors also are relevant - that the story is affirming the possibility of *communication*, that the Gospel can now be *spoken*, beyond the confines of Judaism, to the Gentiles.[13]

10 But this is more likely an internal hiph' il; see above, chapter 1.

11 But the Heb. should more probably be read as "he shall receive a share"; see above, chapter 1.

12 Surely not a reference to prayer or intercession (*contra* Muilenburg, 631), but entirely to his suffering itself (cf. Westermann, 269).

13 F. Bovon, "French Structuralism and Biblical Exegesis", in R. Barthes *et al.*, *Structural Analysis and Biblical Exegesis* (Pittsburgh Theological Monograph Series, 3; Pittsburgh: Pickwick, 1974) 4-20 (17f.).

What is significant about Isa. 53 from this point of view is the *absence* of speech. No communication occurs. No verbal message is conveyed from one *persona* to another. Even if 53:1-11a is to be regarded as "spoken" by the "nations" and "kings" of 52:15, it is not a speech addressed to anyone, and it is certainly not introduced by a verb or formula of speech. A form-critical definition of the passage as "report"[14] is misleading if it ignores the reality that nothing is in fact reported *to* anyone. Similarly, though it is clear that in 52:13-15 and 53:11b-12 Yahweh "speaks", speech-formulas and addressee are equally absent.

The absence of speech as a formal element of the poem is also made concrete in the explicit depiction of the silence of the servant: "he did not open his mouth" (*twice* in 53:7).[15] It is in order to slow the tempo at this momentous statement that the only elaborated simile[16] of the poem is introduced.

Throughout, silence is kept, speech is avoided. The kings are speechless before the servant (52:15). The servant is not addressed by God, withdraws from the society of men (*hᵃdal 'îšîm*, 53:3), and at the moment when some word of protest may have been expected to be uttered - the moment of the unjust judgment passed upon him - silence again rises to the surface of the poem: "who complained or mused aloud on, spoke of (*yᵉśôḥēah*)[17] his fate?" (53:8). Likewise no other *persona* speaks to or is addressed by any other. The only "hearing" has gone on outside the dimension of the poem: the "we" *do* hear *about* something (presumably the servant),

14 As Westermann, 255f.

15 The repetition is not just "the most beautiful and expressive *Nachklang* in the whole writing" (L. Köhler, *Deuterojesaja (Jesaja 40-55) stilkritisch untersucht* [BZAW 37; Giessen: Töpelmann, 1923] 95) - which is an aesthetic judgment - but a symbol of the essential meaning of the poem. It contrasts, perhaps intentionally, with the conventional lament of the innocent sufferer so amply attested in Hebrew psalmic literature.

16 The simile of 53:2 is functional (i.e. the simile itself makes the point about the servant's growth, and is not decorative or elaborative); that of 53:6 would be perfunctory were it not that the image (of the sheep) is identical to that of 53:7, and so plays a contrastive role ("we" as sheep vs. "he" as sheep). In 53:7 the simile is, from a utilitarian point of view, entirely unnecessary (i.e. it adds no new information), so its significance is entirely rhetorical.

17 Clearly a vocal activity, unlike modern "meditation" or "musing". "Gave a thought to", as many modern versions (e.g. NEB) render, makes it too much a mental activity. JB "would any one plead his cause" is on the right lines.

but from whom or what is not clear. What is clear is that what goes on in the poem is a matter of "seeing" (*rāʾû*) what has *not* been "told" (*lōʾ-suppar*) and of "considering" (*hitbônānû*) what has *not* been "heard" (*lōʾ-šāmᵉʿû*). The poem is about seeing, not hearing; so it is about vision rather than verbal communication.

e. Affect analysis

Hebrew poetry is steeped in affective terminology. To fear, hate, be ashamed, sorrow, be angry, rejoice, love, be comforted, have courage, trust, pity are the stuff of psalmic and prophetic language. We have only to glance through the next chapter, Isaiah 54, to find "desolate" (v. 1), "do not fear", "you will not be ashamed", "do not be confounded", "you will not be disappointed", "shame", "reproach" (v. 4), "grieved in spirit" (v. 6), "great compassion" (v. 7), "overflowing wrath", "everlasting love", "I have loved you" (v. 8), "not to be angry", "not to rebuke" (v. 9), "my love", "your lover" (v. 10), "not pitied" (v. 11), "you will not fear", "terror shall not come near you" (v. 14). Several other terms, like "sing" (v.1), "storm-tossed one" (v. 11) also have an emotive connotation. And even more striking than a catalogue of affective verbs would be an analysis of the dynamics of that poem in terms of affects.

What then is the situation in Isaiah 53? To read it again after chapter 54, one is struck by the almost total absence of affective terms. Yahweh does not say how he *feels* about the servant, of the servant himself not a single emotion is expressed, the "we" say nothing of how they feel about "him" except to deny the feeling they once had, while of the "they" it can only be said that if astonishment is an affect, that emotion passes quickly enough.

Yahweh, to be sure, announces the elevation of the servant (52:13) and his own rewarding of him (53:12) - but objectively. The verb *ḥāpēṣ* (53:10) might in most other contexts be read as affective, but here it can hardly mean "Yahweh was delighted/ pleased to crush him"; *ḥāpēṣ* must here be volitional - "he decided, purposed, willed"[18] - just as the noun *ḥēpeṣ* in the same verse must

18 So e.g. RSV "it was the will of the LORD"; "it was Yhwh's purpose" (de Boer, 35); cf. North, 147f., Winton Thomas, 120. Of course, emendation of the following word *dakkᵉʾ⸱* to *dakkāʾô* "his crushed one", which I have rejected as unnecessary, does introduce an affective note into the verb.

44

bear its late meaning of "business", what one sets one's mind to,[19] rather than "pleasure, delight".

On the subject of the servant's interior feelings the poet appears deliberately reticent: our versions try to make amends for the psychological vacuum by making him a "man of sorrows, and acquainted with grief" (AV, RV, RSV), "tormented and humbled by suffering" (NEB) (53:3), but the Hebrew terms *mak'ōbôt* and *ḥŏlî* refer to physical pain[20] and leave the sufferer's inner state undisclosed. What then of the servant's "satisfaction" (*yiśbāʿ*, 53:11)? Has the poet here at last allowed us one glimpse of the servant's emotion? No, not even here, for the verb *śābaʿ* refers throughout the OT to satisfaction in a literal or metaphorical sense, not to affective gratification.[21] In 53:11, in any case, "he is satisfied" (*yiśbāʿ*) seems to be parallel to, or a gloss upon, "he is satiated" (*yir'eh* read as an orthographic variant of *yirweh*, as has been argued above). What he is satiated with is either (i) his "experience" or his "humiliation", i.e. what he has suffered, or (ii), if *yiśbāʿ* is simply a gloss upon *yir'eh*, the "burden of his *nepeš*". The sense is virtually the same in both cases: he has had more than his fill of suffering, but the psychological effect that suffering has upon him is hidden from us by the poet.

The reaction of the "we" to the servant has indeed been expressed in affective terms: "we" did not desire (*ḥāmad*) him (53:2),[22] "he" was despised (*bāzâ*) by men (53:31); and (perhaps) "we" ourselves despised him (53:3b).[23] But these are precisely the feelings

19 So BDB, 343a; cf. Isa. 58:3, 13; Eccl. 3:1,7.

20 Cf. Winton Thomas, 122.

21 Typically, *śābaʿ* means "to have eaten, or drunk enough" (e.g. Ex. 16:12; Deut. 6:11; Isa. 66:11); in a metaphorical sense, "to have enough, or more than enough" (e.g. Ps. 88:4 "My *nepeš* is full of (*śābaʿ*) troubles"; 123:3 "We have had more than enough of contempt" (RSV); Isa. 1:11 "I have had enough of burnt offerings"; similarly Hab. 2:16; Lam. 3:15). Such usages of course signify the very opposite of gratification. Out of a total of nearly 100 occurrences of the verb *śābaʿ*, the only place where a case could be made out for an affective sense is Ps. 17:15 *'eśbeʿâ behāqîṣ temûnāteka*, where however the vision of God's *temûnâ* "form" serves as the satiation of the psalmist's desire by way of contrast with the present satiety of the wicked and their sons (*yiśbeʿû bānîm*, v.14).

22 We could perhaps add "we did not envy him", if Dahood is right in translating *nir'ēhû* thus (p.66).

23 If *wannibzēhû* is to be read (cf. 1QIsᵃ *wnbwzhw*; Pesh. *wštnyhy*; Winton Thomas, 123).

that the "we" have now rejected; their attitude to him now is depicted in language entirely free of emotion.

As for the "they", their "dismay" (*šāmam*, 52:13), which is clearly an affective term, belongs to the conventional language used upon beholding the fate of the wicked.[24] But that also is an emotion they no longer experience, whether because it is they who utter the "confession" of 53:1-11a or because they are the *rabbîm* and the *'aṣûmîm* with whom the servant is to be found dividing the spoil in 53:12. What they then feel about him once again lies beyond the poet's concern.

It would be absurd to suppose that the absence of affective language from the poem is a mark of coldness or clinical detachment. One is reminded rather of the opacity of the narrative of Gen. 22, where Abraham moves in silence, like a sleepwalker or automaton,[25] like one who moves through a vacuum, the journey like a holding of the breath, while the serving men, ass, wood and knife are just that and nothing more, not even admitting of an adjective of description, a word of their origin or usefulness or appearance.[26] Here too nothing must divert the attention from what is going on in the poem: the breaking in of a new vision of the servant and of the nexus of relationships that surround him.

f. Temporal analysis

A certain temporal structure is important in the poem: it is the polarity of "then" and "now" which corresponds to the dualities within the relationships. Thus there is a clear "before" and "after" in the relationship of the "we" to the "he": first we "esteemed him not" (53:3), and then we came to recognize that "he has borne our pains" (53:4). Likewise in the relationship between God and

24 For the idea of "many" (*rabbîm*), or "all", or "all who see" the fate of the wicked or the ruin of a wicked city being "dismayed" (*šāmam*), cf. 1 Kgs. 9:8 // 1 Chr. 7:21; Jer. 18:16; 19:8; 49:17; 50:13; Ezek. 26:16; 27:35; 28:19; 32:9f. On the possible connection of this idea with treaty terminology, see D.R. Hillers, *Treaty-Curses and the Old Testament Prophets* (Bib Or 16; Rome: Pontifical Biblical Institute, 1964) 76f.; see also Hillers, "A Convention in Hebrew Literature: The Reaction to Bad News", *ZAW* 77 (1965) 86-90.

25 Cf. G.W. Coats, "Abraham's Sacrifice of Faith. A Form-Critical Study of Genesis 22", *Interp* 27 (1973) 389-400 (397).

26 Cf. E. Auerbach, *Mimesis. The Representation of Reality in Western Literature* (Princeton: University Press, 1953) 9f.

the servant: plainly Yahweh's deciding to "put him to grief"
(53:10) precedes his "dividing him a portion with the great" (53:
12). Similarly in the "they" - "he" relationship, "they" are at first
"astonished" (52:14) and "startled" (52:15) by the servant, but
then he is proved innocent in their sight (53:11), and they have
their sins "borne" by him (53:11,12).

This temporal structure is not, however, expressed - as might
be expected - by means of the Hebrew tenses. In the "we" - "he"
relationship, the "before" and "after" are both depicted with perfect tense verbs. In the "they" - "he" relationship both perfect
and imperfect are used for the "before" (52:14, 15; 53:11 [*yisbōl*]; 53:12 [*yapgîaʻ*]) and the "after" (52:15 [*rāʼû; hitbônānû*]);
53:12 [*yᵉhallēq*]); even in 52:14-15, where the perfects correspond to the "before" and the imperfects in the principal clause
correspond to the "after", it is not the tenses, or at least not the
tenses alone, that indicate temporality; it is the comparison (which
can only be understood as a contrast)[27] between the "as" (*kaʼᵃšer*)
of v. 14 and the "so" (*kēn*) of v. 15.[28] Only in the relationship between Yahweh and the servant does the perfect tense happen to
correspond with the "before" and the imperfect with the "after"
(52:13; 53:10-12).

There are other indicators as well that the contrast of *qtl/yqtl*
verb forms does not indicate temporal sequence. In 53:7 we have,
in what appears to be, from the perspective of the poem, a narrative of past completed events, the perfect *niggaś*, "he was smitten",
the participle *naʻaneh*,[29] "humbled" and the imperfect *yiptaḥ* "he
opened" (twice); *yûbāl* "he was led", is also an *yqtl* form which
most probably belongs to the narrative sequence,[30] while the *qtl*
form *neʼᵉlāmâ* also possibly does.[31] Similarly in 53:12 the three

27 It is pointless to compare the astonishment of the many (v.14) with the startling and
the astonished silence of the many nations and kings (v.15).

28 That is, there is no other significant point of contrast between the two classes;
Dahood misses the temporal contrast by taking *kēn* as an emphatic (pp. 63,65).

29 Emended by some to the perfect *naʻanâ* (cf. Winton Thomas, 123).

30 The final phrase *wᵉlōʼ yiptaḥ pih* must link with *yûbāl*, which can therefore not
belong to the simile (so KJV, NEB; McKenzie, 130; contra RV, RSV, JB, JPS;
North, 65).

31 Most take *rāḥēl* to be the subject, but some emend the verb to *neʼᵉlām* to make the
servant the subject (cf. North, 229) or take *neʼᵉlāmâ* as an archaic third masculine
singular perfect (Dahood, 68). NAB and Westermann, 254, have "he was silent" - on
what grounds is unclear.

qtl forms referring to the history of the servant (*he^{ᶜᵉ}râ, nimnâ, nāśâ*) are followed by a *yqtl* (*yapgîaᶜ*) plainly belonging to the same sequence.

Again, in 53:10,11 the offering of the servant's life as a sacrifice for others and his "bearing iniquities" (*'im tāśîm 'ăśām napšô; ᶜᵃwōnātām hû' yisbōl*) is portrayed with *yqtl* verbs, while elsewhere in the poem *qtl* verbs are used (e.g. 53:4 *nāśā'; sᵉbālām*) for the same activity.

These factors make it impossible to establish any systematic correspondence between the Hebrew "tenses" used in the poem and the poem's own temporal structure.[32] From the poem itself we cannot determine *when* its various elements take place; that is, whether everything in the poem is viewed by the poet as prior to, contemporaneous with, or later than his own time, or distributed throughout those various segments of time. Perhaps from the *context* of the poem some of these questions can be answered, but my concern here, as I have remarked earlier, is to let the poem speak for itself without the imposition of a frame of reference derived from outside the poem. From the poem itself it cannot be asserted, for example, that the imperfects of 52:13 or 53:10ff. must be translated as futures rather than presents, or that the perfect of 52:14a is prior to the poet's time, the imperfects of 52:15a are later than his time, while the perfects of 52:15b are really future perfects, referring to a time later than that of the poem's composition, but earlier than that of v. 15a.

This does not mean, however, that no temporal sequence can be discerned in the poem. Most significant is the fact that the narrative of the servant's history begins and ends with *wyqtl* forms (waw consecutive plus the "imperfect"): *wayyaᶜ al* (53:2) and *wayyittēn* (53:8). No clearer indication of narrative form is needed in Hebrew;[33] the verbs bounded by these two narrative verb forms are meant therefore to be read as a narrative sequence that begins with the servant's growing up and ends with the preparation of his tomb. By a criterion of coherence 53:12b, c, for example, must refer to the time of 53:2-8.[34] By the criterion of the "before" -

32 This observation I find confirmed only by Dahood (pp. 65,72).

33 Of course, we cannot infer that the poet regards the history as having already occurred.

34 Hence *yapgîaᶜ* is a preterite, and NAB is unlikely: "And he shall take away the sins of many, and win pardon for their offenses".

48

"after" polarity, the success of the servant (52:13; 53:12a) must follow the time of his suffering, but there is no reason within the poem to project the moment of success into the time that is as yet future to the poet.

In sum, the poem does not entitle us to structure a sequence of past, present and future, but only a polarity of "before" and "after". Attention is focussed almost entirely on the relationships of the *personae* and the alterations that occur in those relationships. The only temporal structure that can be plotted corresponds to, and is in fact only discerned by means of, the relational changes.

4.   DONE BY SAYING : LANGUAGE AS EVENT

4. Done by saying: language as event

Our study hitherto suggests that some approach to Isa. 53 other than that of conventional historical criticism will be appropriate. Not only has the historical-critical method failed to provide acceptable solutions for the enigmas of the poem, but also our close reading of the poem's rhetoric has ruled out any merely objectivist approach to its meaning.

The outlook of the "new hermeneutic" school provides, I suggest, a framework within which some kind of justice may be done to the character and quality of this poem. A brief sketch of some aspects of the new hermeneutic particularly appropriate for our study thus seems to be called for.[1]

1. The new hermeneutic stresses that language can become event; that is, that language need not be mere talk *about* something, but that it can itself *do* something. E. Fuchs therefore commonly uses the term *Sprachereignis* "language event" for this understanding of language.[2] And G. Ebeling remarks: "We do not get at the nature of words by asking what they contain, but by asking what they effect, what they set going".[3]

2. This notion of language as *doing* - which goes against the conventional contrast between speech and action, between *logos* and *praxis* - is parallel, as Robert W. Funk has pointed out,[4] to the concept developed by J.L. Austin of "performative utterances", in which "the issuing of the utterance is the performing of an action".[5] Some well-known examples mentioned by Austin are: "I name this ship the *Queen Elizabeth*", "I give my watch to my brother" (in a will), "I bet you sixpence it will rain tomorrow".[6] Fuchs sim-

1 I am much indebted to my colleague A.C. Thiselton for stimulating my interest in this approach to Biblical interpretation and for clarifying many issues. Of special value have been his papers, "The New Hermeneutic" in *New Testament Interpretation* (ed. I.H. Marshall; Exeter: Paternoster, 1976), and "The Parables as Language Event: Some Comments on Fuchs's Hermeneutics in the Light of Linguistic Philosophy", *SJT* 23 (1970) 437-68.

2 E. Fuchs, *Hermeneutik* (4th edn.; Tübingen: Mohr, 1970) 131; cf. R.W. Funk, *Language, Hermeneutic, and Word of God* (New York: Harper and Row, 1966) 51.

3 G. Ebeling, *The Nature of Faith* (London: Collins, 1961) 137.

4 *Language, Hermeneutic, and Word of God* 26f.

5 *How to do Things with Words* (2nd edn., ed. J.O. Urmson and M. Sbisà; Oxford: Clarendon Press, 1975).

6 Austin, *op. cit.* 5.

ilarly points out that to name a man "brother" performatively is thereby to admit him into a brotherly relationship.[7] Austin of course is interested primarily in performative utterances in ordinary language, Fuchs and Ebeling in "speech-events" in kerygmatic language, especially in the language of Jesus and in particular within his parabolic utterances, while I am interested in this functional aspect of literary language in general, and of high poetry in particular.

3. The next question concerns the *way* in which the language of parable or poem can be event. Here Austin's interest must of course drop out of sight, since he has established simply that one conventional use of language is as deed, thus providing the basic and irrefutable foundation for the more sophisticated superstructure of hermeneutical theory.

The *way* in which language is event is by its creating of an alternative *world* and thereby destroying the universal validity of the conventional "world". Thus Fuchs speaks of language as "world-forming and world-destroying".[8] "World" can be defined as "the total set of perception and participation in which we exist, the locus of historical being".[9] A literary text creates an alternative "world", another set of principles, values, relationships, and perceptions, which then confronts the reader. The result is a conflict between two worlds, two ways of seeing things, which puts the ball into the reader's court.

4. The world thus created invites the reader to enter it. It is not a world that can be viewed objectively, from the outside, as a spectator. One needs to be a participant in it, to experience it, in order to understand it. This is the way to more than mere knowledge (*Erkenntnis*), as H.G. Gadamer points out;[10] it leads to "understanding" (*Verstehen*), which is reached through "modes of experience in which truth comes to light" (*Erfahrungsweisen*) as one is

---

7 *Studies of the Historical Jesus* (London: SCM, 1964) 209.

8 Quoted by W.G. Doty, *Contemporary New Testament Interpretation* (Englewood Cliffs, N.J.: Prentice-Hall, 1972) 42. C.S. Lewis speaks of the "unmaking of your mind" in a similar connection (*An Experiment in Criticism* [Cambridge: Cambridge University Press, 1961] 139).

9 Doty, *op. cit.* 37.

10 H.-G. Gadamer, *Truth and Method* (New York: Seabury, 1975). See also Thiselton, "Parables as Language Event" 443f., and cf. Lewis, *Experiment in Criticism* 139.

taken hold of by creative language or art. Unless one "enters" the alternative world created by language one cannot be gripped by its reality, but is condemned to remain a spectator. Gadamer is thinking of the analogy of a game, whose *reality* is experienced only by the players, and not by the spectators - however much they may know about its theory.

5. The process of moving from the one "world" to the other has been strikingly termed by Gadamer a "merging of horizons" (*Horizontverschmelzung*).[11] One cannot abandon overnight one's original world, because it is only in that world that one has one's bearings and knows therefore one's own identity at the intersection of a three-dimensional grid of space and time and personal relationships. But also the "other" world may not sometimes be anything more than another perspective on the original world.

Hence the significance of the simile of "horizons". A.C. Thiselton has expressed Gadamer's concept of horizons thus:

> When language brings a new "world" into existence, the hearer who enters this world becomes aware of new horizons of meaning. But these necessarily differ from the horizons of understanding which have hitherto marked the extent of his own world. Thus, to begin with, two different worlds stand over against each other, each with its own horizon. Yet the peculiarity of horizons is that their positions are variable, in accordance with the position from which they are viewed. Hence adjustments can be made in the hearer's own understanding until the two horizons come to merge into one. A new comprehensive horizon now appears, which serves as the boundary of an enlarged world of integrated understanding.[12]

6. When the text is seen as creating a world which the reader is invited to "enter",[13] it becomes obvious that the conventional model of the relation between a text and its interpreter has been made obsolete. No longer can it be said of a text such as poem or parable (though it may still properly be said of a legal document or technical manual or business letter) that it is the "object" of scrutiny by the "subject" (the interpreter) - the familiar Cartesian dis-

11 Gadamer, *Truth and Method* 269-73.

12 Thiselton, "Parables as Language Event" 445.

13 C.S. Lewis speaks of "cross[ing] the frontier into a new region" in the same connection (*Experiment in Criticism*).

tinction - but that the text as language-event, world-creating and world-destroying, has the primacy over the interpreter. As James M. Robinson has put it:

> The flow of the traditional relation between subject and object, in which the subject interrogates the object, and, if he masters it, obtains from it his answer, has been significantly reversed. For it is now the object - which should henceforth be called the subject matter - that puts the subject [the interpreter] in question.[14]

It is significant that it is precisely in relation to art (the plastic or literary work of art) that it becomes clear that the categories of subject and object must be transcended. As Heidegger argued, if the dualist subject-object perspective is adopted, either art is reduced to the realm of the purely sensual, in which case it cannot be said to reveal truth; or else it is elevated into the realm of intellectual concepts, in which case it becomes reduced to the level of aesthetics.[15] Literary critics have, indeed, often recognized the primacy of the work of art, which interprets the critic rather than being interpreted *by* the critic, as the following remark shows:

> The first demand any work of any art makes upon us is surrender. Look. Listen. Receive. Get yourself out of the way.[16]

7. Another way of putting the relationship of the world of the text and the interpreter as "actively assum[ing] one of the concrete roles which it offers him". The interpreter is then "carried forward by a kind of inner logic of consequences which the chosen role brings with it."[17]

14 *The New Hermeneutic* (ed. J.M. Robinson and J.B. Cobb; New Frontiers in Theology, 2; New York: Harper and Row, 1964) 23f.

15 A.C. Thiselton kindly drew my attention to this point. Heidegger's essay "The Origin of the Work of Art" is translated in *Philosophies of Art and Beauty* (ed. A. Hofstadter and R. Kuhns; New York: Random House, 1964).

16 Lewis, *Experiment in Criticism* 19.

17 Thiselton, "Parables as Language Event" 441.

5.   SAID AND DOING : ISAIAH 53 AS LANGUAGE-EVENT

5. Said and doing: Isaiah 53 as language-event

The relevance of the foregoing sketch for our understanding of
Isa. 53 is doubtless already obvious; nevertheless, some points of
contact should perhaps be spelled out.

a. The impasse of historical-critical scholarship in the face of
the enigmas of the poem can function heuristically in directing
our attention away from a sense of "the poem as problem" to the
poem as language-event.

It is remarkable that Old Testament scholarship has never made
such a step, but has almost without exception taken an apparently
masochistic delight in the intractability of the "problems" of the
poem, as if it were primarily a brain-teaser, a puzzle for the most
advanced students. Only Claus Westermann has recognised the in-
sensitivity of such an approach, and has vigorously denied that
quests for "identification" - i.e. problem-solving enquiries - are
appropriate.[1] The language of the servant songs, he says, "at once
reveals and conceals the servant."

> The veiled manner of speaking is intentional . . . Exegesis must
> then be conscious of the limit thus imposed, and be careful to
> call a halt at those places where the distinctive nature of the
> songs demands this . . . On principle, their exegesis must not be
> controlled by the question, 'Who is this servant of God?' . . .
> Precisely this is what they neither tell nor intend to tell us. The
> questions which should control exegesis are: 'What do the texts
> make known about what transpires, or is to transpire, between
> God, the servant, and those to whom his task pertains?'[2]

Westermann thus bars the way to a false path, but his suggestion
of another direction in which exegesis should strike out is still too
fixated by the concept of the text as information.

b. Once it is recognised that the text does not exist as a carrier
of information, but has a life of its own, it becomes impossible to
talk of *the* meaning of a text, as if it had only *one* proper meaning.
Recognition of the hermeneutical circle, in which meaning is seen
to reside not in the text but in what the text becomes for the

1 Westermann, 20.
2 Westermann, 93.

reader, also leads to the legitimacy of *multiple meanings*.[3]

A similar conclusion is reached, quite independently of the "new hermeneutic" school, by literary critics who stress, to one degree or another, the "autonomy of the work of art". While it is too extreme, I believe, to regard a literary work of art as totally autonomous of its author, and consequently to be understood independently of the circumstances of its origin,[4] there is truth in L. Alonso-Schökel's remark that when an author produces a work the umbilical cord has to be cut and the work must go forth into the world on its own. Thus the original author's meaning, which is what is generally meant by *the* meaning of the text,[5] is by no means the only meaning a text may legitimately have (or rather, create). We cannot even be sure that a literary text (or any work of art) "originally" - whenever that was - meant one thing and one thing only to its author; even the author may have had multiple meanings in mind.

We may therefore prepare ourselves to recognize various meanings that our text, Isa. 53, can create. When, for example, Philip the evangelist "begins" at that scripture and preaches Christ to the Ethiopian eunuch, we should not think so much of a *re-application* of the prophetic text which once meant something quite different, but of one of the vast variety of meanings the text itself can create. The text creates a world in which participants in the world of the text get to know their way around, and come to be able to say, like Wittgenstein, "Now I can go on".

Similarly we may reconcile ourselves to *not wishing* to identify the persons or groups of the fifth century B.C. to which the text may have alluded. Of course, if, for example, the "servant" is a code-name for Deutero-Isaiah, and his deliverance from "death" is a poetic expression for release from a Babylonian prison, and so on,

3   Cf. T.S. Eliot's remark that the meaning of a poem is "what the poem means to different sensitive readers" ("The Frontiers of Criticism", in *On Poetry and Poets* [London: Faber and Faber 1957] 113).

4   See, for example, E. Staiger, *Die Kunst der Interpretation* (4th edn.; Zürich: Atlantis, 1963); M. Weiss, "Wege der neuen Dichtungswissenschaft in ihrer Auswendung auf die Psalmenforschung", *Bib* 42 (1961) 255-302 (259); Palmer, *Hermeneutics* 246f. For criticism of this approach, see for example Helen Gardner, *The Business of Criticism* (Oxford: Clarendon Press, 1959) 17-23.

5   See, for example, E.D. Hirsch, *Validity in Interpretation* (New Haven: Yale University Press, 1967).

all other interpretations of the poem are *quite wrong*. On the understanding advanced here, it is not a matter of being quite wrong or even quite right: there are only more and less appropriate interpretations, no doubt, according to how well the world of the poem comes to expression in the new situation.

c. The poem is free to do its work by its very lack of specificity, its openness to a multiplicity of readings.

Of course, that lack of specificity, the enigmatic quality of the poem *could* perhaps be simply a historical accident. It *could* be that once there was a key to the enigmas of the poem, and that that key has been lost, so that *we* can never know what the poem means precisely and exactly - and, on this view, truly. Perhaps a line has dropped out at the beginning of ch. 53 which made clear who the "we" were;[6] perhaps it was "obvious" to the "original audience" (to use the language familiar to an unliterary historical-critical scholarship) who the servant was; perhaps in that case it was equally plain what the nature of his sufferings was, and whether he underwent death or not. Perhaps too it was clear whether his mission extended to the Gentiles or only to Israelites of the dispersion.

May it not be, however - and does not this approach respect the integrity of the text rather more than a circle of cautious "perhapses"? - that the enigmas are part of what the poem must be in order to be itself? That is, that it exists to create another world, a world indeed that is recognizably our own, with brutality and suffering and God and a coming-to-see on the part of some, but not a world that simply once existed and is gone for good. The poem's very lack of specificity refuses to let it be tied down to one spot on the globe, or frozen at one point in history: it opens up the possibility that the poem can become true in a variety of circumstances - that is its work.

d. The world which the poem creates is a topsy-turvy world when judged by ordinary human standards.[7]

It is a world where a servant (*or*, slave) is elevated above kings, to the consternation of conventional wisdom; compare Prov. 19:10:

6 So, for example, Whitehouse, 199.

7 This is made clear within the poem itself, which speaks of its own message as "something never heard before" (52:15).

"It is not fitting for a fool to live in luxury,
    much less for a servant to rule over princes."
It is a world where *one* achieves what the *many* cannot, and where
the "intercession" of one avails for the many (53:12). It is a world
where, so the poem makes out, the man God designates as his servant and as a hero is an object of loathing, so disfigured that he
looks sub-human (*mošhat mē'îš mar'ēhû*, 52:14).[8] In this world,
it is assumed with none too delicate irony, a man who serves God
by "practising non-violence and never speaking dishonestly" (53:9)
inevitably finds himself in the condemned cell (note the force of
ʿ*al* in 53:9b). Here too it is taken for granted in a mere half verse
that the suffering of a righteous man is the will of God (53:10a),
a breach with conventional theology so drastic that elsewhere a
whole book is devoted to its ramifications (Job). So the social
order, the strength of numbers, good taste, ordinary human de-
cency, and the justice of God are all in turn called into question
by this topsy-turvy, not to say shocking, poem.

This is the world that the reader is bidden to give his assent to -
or rather, to enter. It is not an obviously appealing invitation. To
allow the horizon of the poem to "merge" with any conventional
horizon would almost seem to call for standing on one's head. But
this is a poem precisely about horizons: it concerns perspectives,
the way one *sees*, as we have noted above. It sets forth a vision of
the world which is radically different from our prior expectations;
it is a new "world" in that its scale of values differ from the conventional.

e. The means by which the reader of the poem is able to enter
the world of the poem is by identification with the *personae* of
the poem, that is, by an assumption of one of the roles presented
in the poem.

If one identifies with the "they", who find the history of the
servant unbelievable and his aspect revolting, one is still on the
edge of the poem's world, an observer looking in on it but not
committed to it. Yet the "they" are at least aware of the servant;
they "see" and "ponder" the servant's fate. Though repelled, they

8 The figure of Achilles, "bloom of the heroes, who grew up like a sprouting shoot,
   nourished like a plant in the luxuriant earth" (Iliad 18.437f.) is a convenient point of
   reference in the "real" world. Still closer to hand is Krt, "the beautiful one, servant
   of El" (*nʿmn ǵlm 'el*).

are at the same time fascinated by the servant, so they have made the first step towards the way of the servant. What is more, those who identify with the "they" of the poem find, by the time they reach 53:11f, that the servant proves in their presence (*lārabbîm*) to be innocent and to have borne punishment on behalf of them, the many (*ḥēṭ' rabbîm nāśā'*).

If one accepts that the suffering of the innocent is in any way because of, for the sake of, or on behalf of, oneself who deserves to suffer, then one has joined the ranks of the "we". They are the group who once felt like the "they" but have had their eyes opened to the true relationship between themselves and the servant: "he was pierced because of our rebelliousness" (53:5). Identification with the "we" puts one entirely within the world of the poem; it involves a recognition that things are not what they seem and that one can have been dreadfully mistaken about the identity and nature of the true servant of the Lord. It requires also a questioning in order to discover who and where is the servant of Yahweh for oneself. No one can enter the world of the poem without becoming a participant in that world; no one truly understands who the "we" are and what they mean to say unless one has shared their experience of revulsion towards and rejection of the servant and their experience of "conversion", i.e. their recognition of being mistaken, their assurance that the servant is for them *the* significant other and not an insignificant being, despised and rejected.

There is yet another role in the poem which the reader is invited to assume: that of the servant himself. Naturally, if the servant *is* Deutero-Isaiah or some other historical figure, one may empathize with the servant; but I am arguing that the poem's lack of specificity about the servant's identity enables a relationship between the servant and the reader that is deeper than empathy to come into being. It is not simply that the reader may, by exercise of a vivid imagination, put himself in the servant's shoes, and empathetically share the servant's experience. It is rather that the figure of the servant presented by the poem has the potency to reach out from the confines of a historical past and from the poem itself and to "seize" the reader and bend him to a new understanding of himself and of the direction of his life. The reader can, in the presence of this, the central *persona* of the poem, cease to be the active subject interrogating the text, and become the one who is questioned and changed by the text. It is the same case if the servant is, not a historical personage, but an ideal figure. Here again, the force of the poem is not simply to invite the reader to approximate his behaviour and life-style to that of the servant as best he can; it is rather that the figure of the servant seizes, imposes itself upon, a reader - with or without the reader's assent (so this is not the same thing as empathy) - and insists upon interpreting the reader rather than being interpreted by the reader. The assumption of the servant's role becomes, not the voluntary act of a dramatic role-playing, but a compulsion by the figure of the servant. The language becomes more than a tool for the conveyance of information or even emotion; it creates an event: it destroys a world and replaces it by a new one which it brings into being.

f. Cannot something more specific be said about the nature of this figure of the servant?

It can, but not perhaps in the style of an academic paper; perhaps only the language of testimony or confession, which the "we" of the poem find themselves using, can properly express what the servant is, for that means: what the servant is *for me*. Others are questioned and changed by different facets of the servant figure, but for me what is most compelling is that the servant of Yahweh in Isaiah 53 *does nothing and says nothing but lets everything happen to him.* We saw above, in looking at the verbal pattern of the poem (chapter 3c), that the servant is acted upon more often than he acts. Even his "actions" are by turns negative ("he did not open his mouth") or passive ("he bore the punishment"). There is, as we saw, no concrete action done by the servant; he suffers. Even his "intervention" (*yapgîaʿ*, 53:12) for the rebellious, and his "carrying" of punishment (*nāśāʾ, sābal,* 53:4, 11, 12), his "exposing" himself to death (*heʿᵉrâ,* 53:12), are nothing more than his suffering; they are not the acts of a Superman intervening at the critical moment, of an Atlas carrying the world-guilt on his shoulders, of a hero of the trenches exposing himself to enemy fire. They are: his letting everything happen to him.

And, he says nothing (cf. above, chapter 3d): he does not open his mouth. What kind of silence that is I do not well know, for it is so rare in our world. It is not Stoic silence or insolent silence; it is not dumb brutish silence or dumbfounded amazed silence; it is not heroic silence, for he has no one to betray by his speech, but neither is it the silence of ignorance, for he knows what he is doing. It can only be the silence of suffering, his speech and his action mysteriously but deliberately absent.

In a religious culture such as our own, where commitment is measured almost quantitatively by speech and action, the servant of the Lord of Isaiah 53 is ill at ease, for his commitment to the "purposes of Yahweh" (53:10) lies entirely in his silent and unresisting suffering. No one wants to claim that there are no other servants of the Lord except this one of Isaiah 53, that this poem-parable is the only glimpse we have of the reality of servanthood. But this servant still walks among us, wordlessly calling in question our images of servanthood and with his suffering reproaching our easy activisms.